Easy Piano

Good Ol' Southern Gospel

29 TRADITIONAL SONGS OF FAITH

CONTENTS

2	AMAZING GRACE
5	BRINGING IN THE SHEAVES
8	CHURCH IN THE WILDWOOD
10	DO LORD
16	DWELLING IN BEULAH LAND
13	HIS EYE IS ON THE SPARROW
18	I HAVE DECIDED TO FOLLOW JESUS
22	IN THE GARDEN
19	JUST A CLOSER WALK WITH THEE
24	JUST OVER IN THE GLORYLAND
28	LEANING ON THE EVERLASTING ARMS
30	LIFE'S RAILWAY TO HEAVEN
32	THE LILY OF THE VALLEY
25	THE OLD RUGGED CROSS
34	OLD TIME RELIGION
36	ON JORDAN'S STORMY BANKS
38	PRECIOUS MEMORIES
40	ROCK OF AGES
42	SHALL WE GATHER AT THE RIVER?
44	SINCE JESUS CAME INTO MY HEART
46	SWEET BY AND BY
60	SWEET HOUR OF PRAYER
48	THERE IS A FOUNTAIN
50	THERE IS POWER IN THE BLOOD
52	WE'LL UNDERSTAND IT BETTER BY AND BY
54	WHAT A FRIEND WE HAVE IN JESUS
56	WHEN THE ROLL IS CALLED UP YONDER
58	WHEN WE ALL GET TO HEAVEN
61	WHISPERING HOPE

ISBN 978-0-634-00600-5

HAL•LEONARD®
CORPORATION

7777 W. BLUEMOUND RD. P.O. BOX 13819 MILWAUKEE, WI 53213

Visit Hal Leonard Online at
www.halleonard.com

AMAZING GRACE

Words by JOHN NEWTON
Traditional American Melody

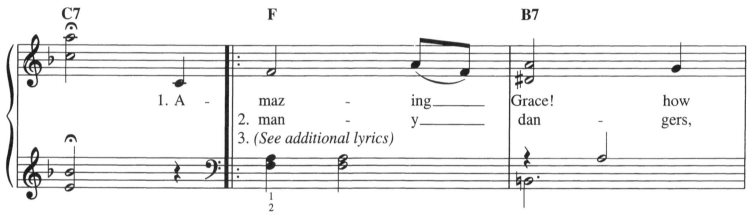

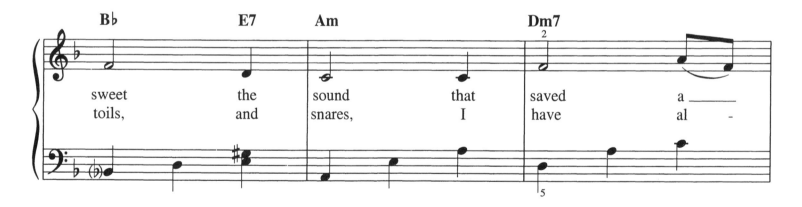

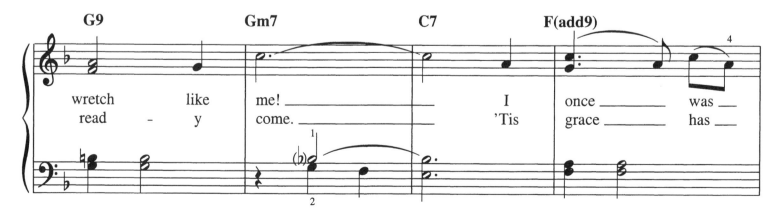

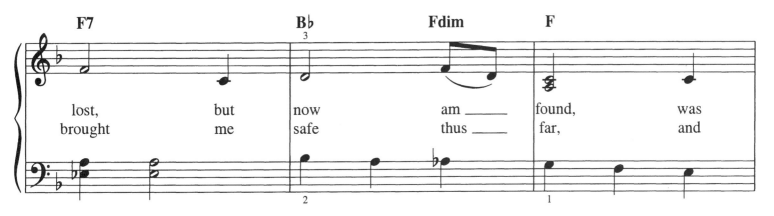

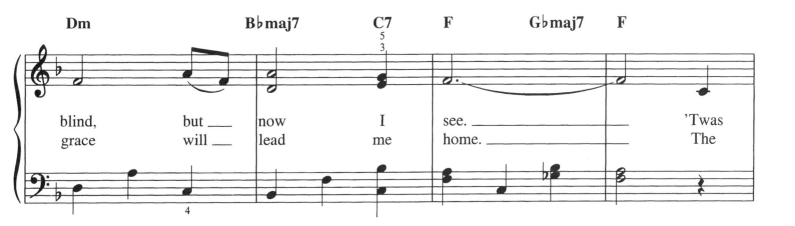

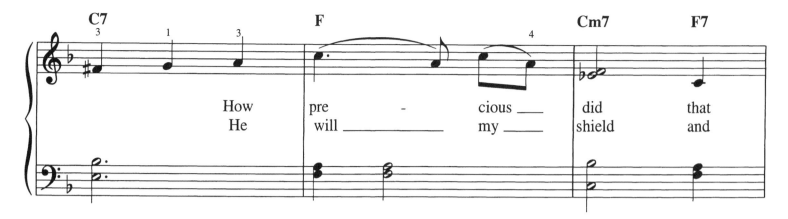

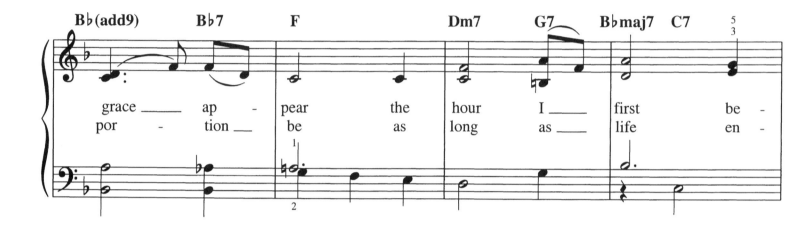

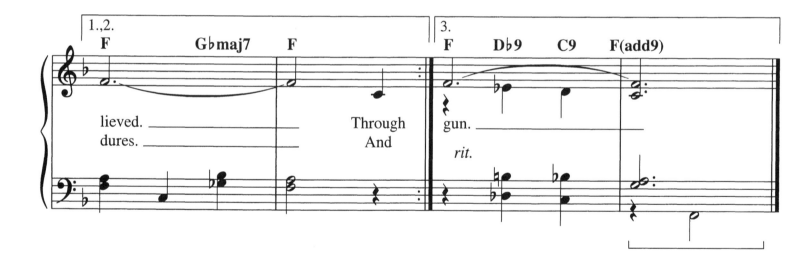

Additional Lyrics

3. And when this flesh and heart shall fail
   and mortal life shall cease.
   I shall possess within the veil
   a life of joy and peace.
   When we've been there ten thousand years,
   bright shining as the sun
   We've no less days to sing God's praise
   than when we first begun.

BRINGING IN THE SHEAVES

Words by KNOWLES SHAW
Music by GEORGE A. MINOR

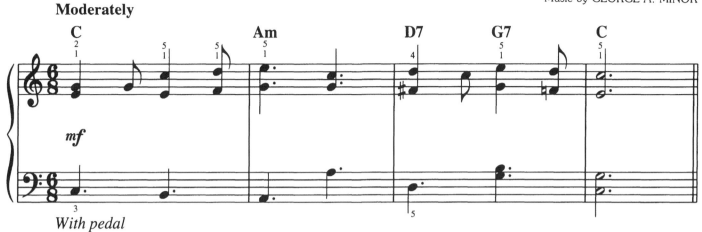

Moderately

mf

With pedal

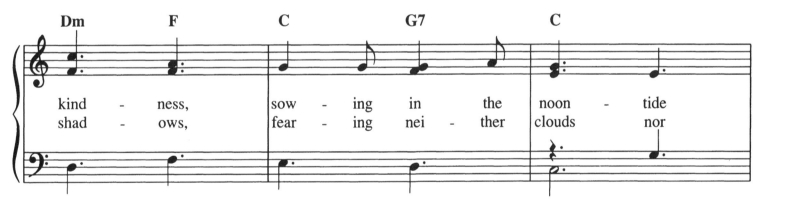

1. Sow - ing in the morn - ing, sow - ing seeds of
2. Sow - ing in the sun - shine, sow - ing in the
3. *(See additional verse)*

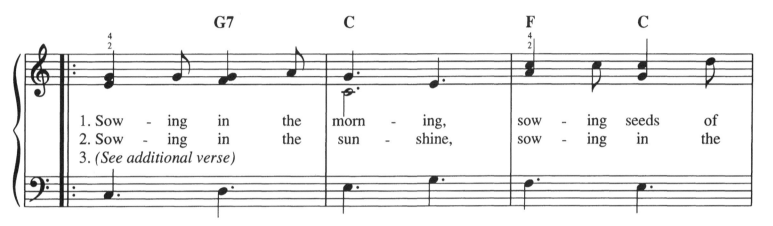

kind - ness, sow - ing in the noon - tide
shad - ows, fear - ing nei - ther clouds nor

and the dew - y eve. Wait - ing for the
win - ter's chill - ing breeze. By and by the

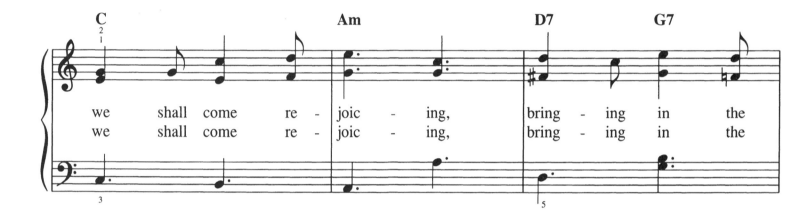

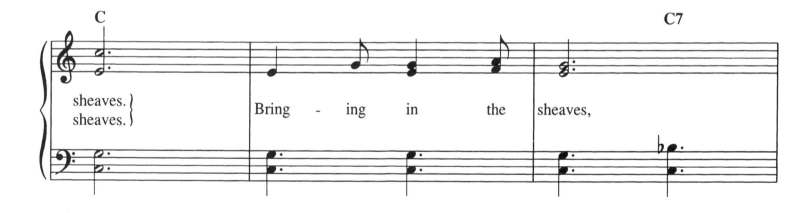

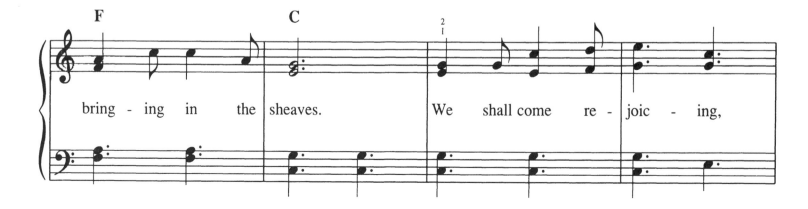

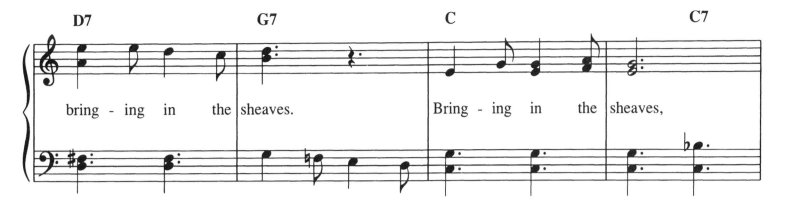

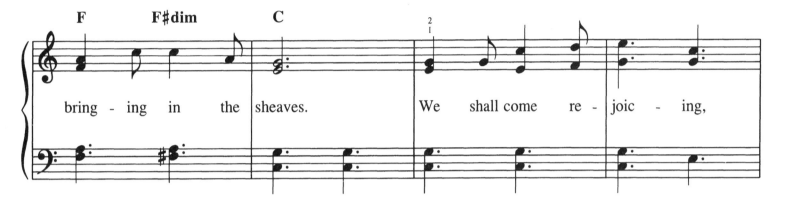

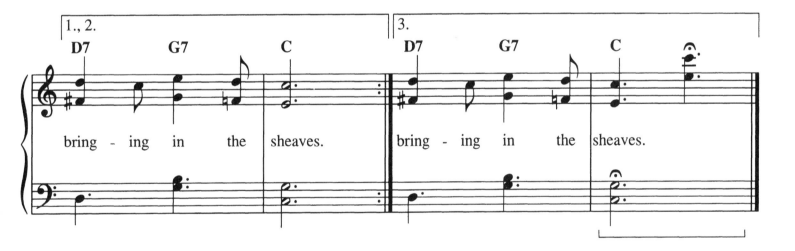

Additional Verse

3. Going forth with weeping, sowing for the Master,
tho' the loss sustained our spirit often grieves.
When our weeping's over, he will bid us welcome,
we shall come rejoicing, bringing in the sheaves.

CHURCH IN THE WILDWOOD

Words and Music by
WILLIAM S. PITTS

Moderate steady beat

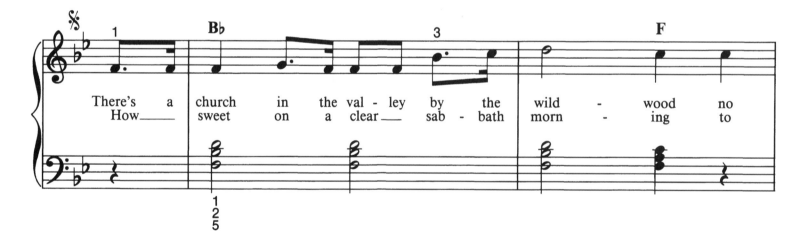

There's a church in the val-ley by the wild - wood no
How___ sweet on a clear___ sab-bath morn - ing to

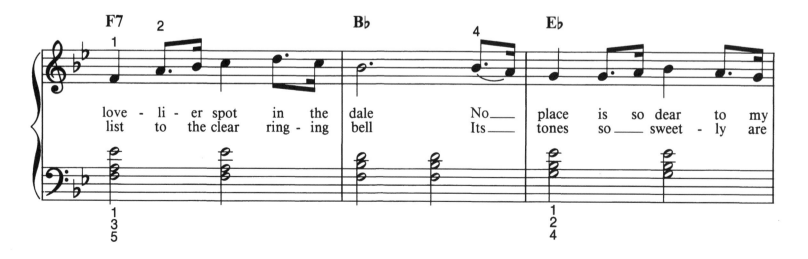

love - li - er spot in the dale
list to the clear ring - ing bell

No___ place is so dear to my
Its___ tones so___ sweet-ly are

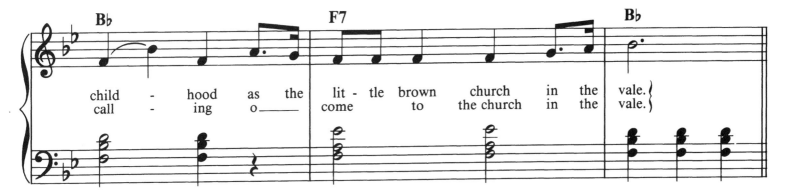

DO LORD

Traditional

Moderately

I've got a home in
I took Je - sus

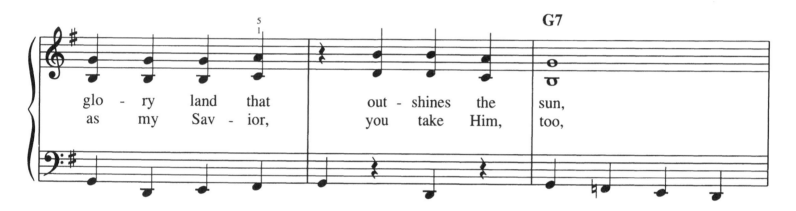

glo - ry land that
as my Sav - ior,

out - shines the
you take Him,

sun,
too,

I've got a home in
I took Je - sus

glo - ry - land that
as my Sav - ior,

out - shines the
you take Him,

sun,
too,

I've got a home in
I took Je - sus

glo - ry - land that
as my Sav - ior,

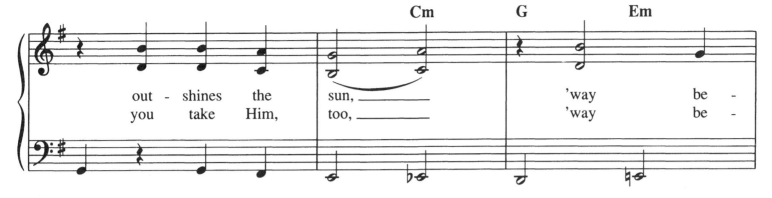

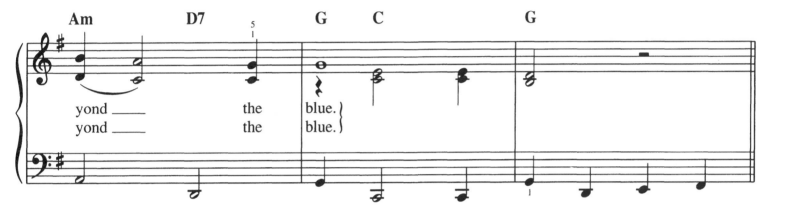

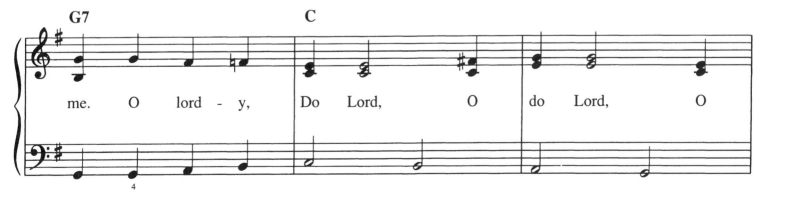

do re-mem-ber me, Do Lord, O

do Lord, O do re-mem-ber me, _____

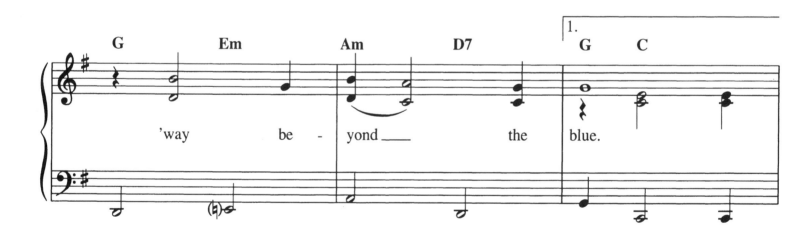

'way be-yond _____ the blue.

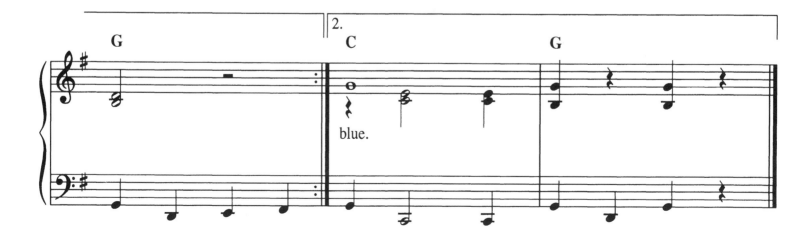

blue.

HIS EYE IS ON THE SPARROW

Text by CIVILLA D. MARTIN
Music by CHARLES H. GABRIEL

Warmly

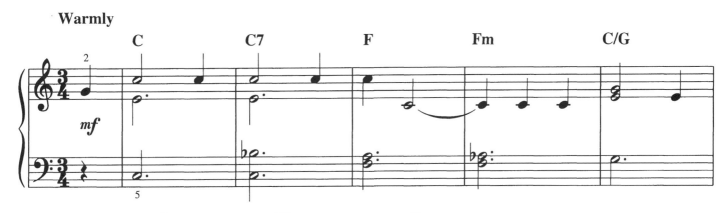

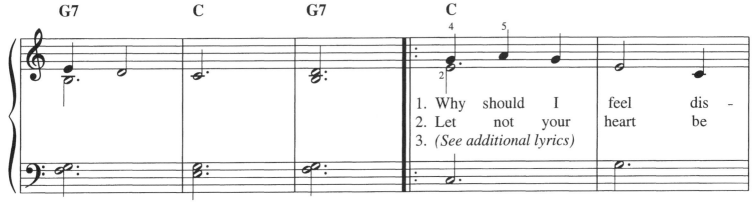

1. Why should I feel dis be-
2. Let not your heart be
3. *(See additional lyrics)*

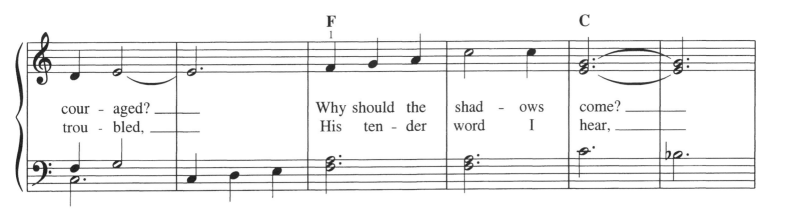

cour - aged? ____ Why should the shad - ows come? ____
trou - bled, ____ His ten - der word I hear, ____

Why should my heart be lone - ly, ____ and long for
And rest - ing on His good - ness, ____ I lose my

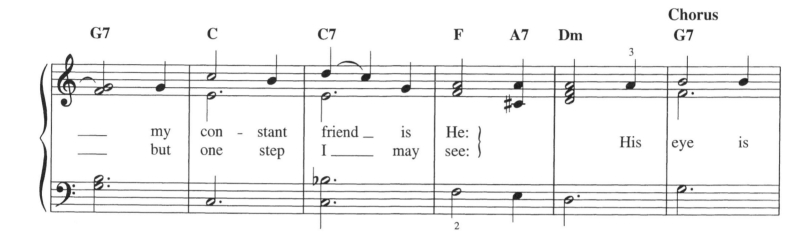

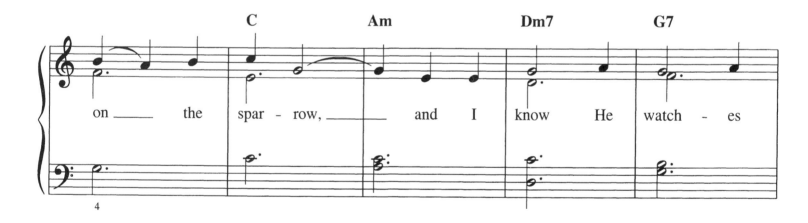

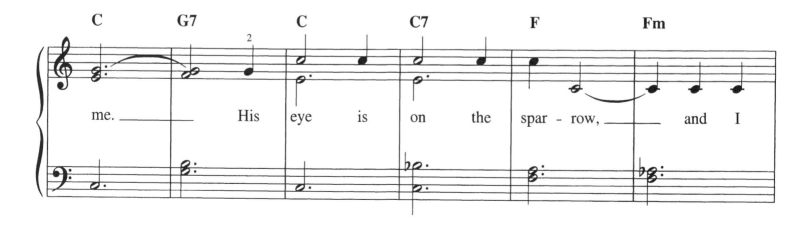

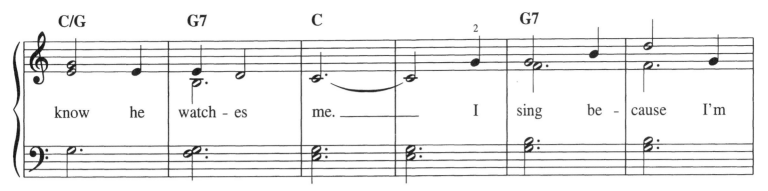

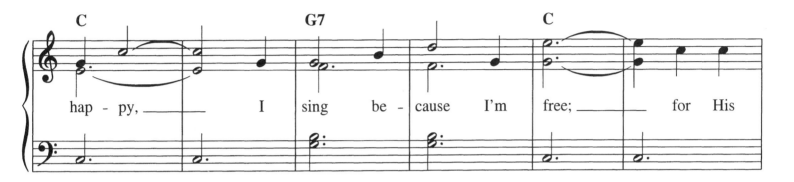

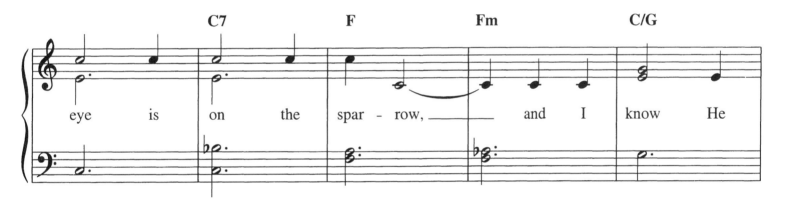

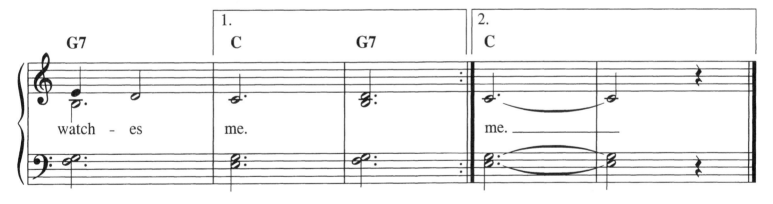

Additional Lyrics

3. Whenever I am tempted,
   Whenever clouds arise.
   When song gives place to sighing,
   When hope within me dies.
   I draw the closer to Him,
   From care He sets me free:
   Chorus

DWELLING IN BEULAH LAND

Words and Music by
C. AUSTIN MILES

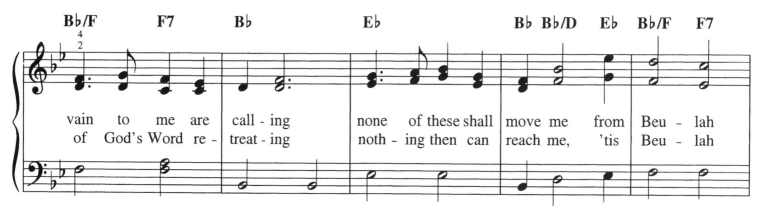

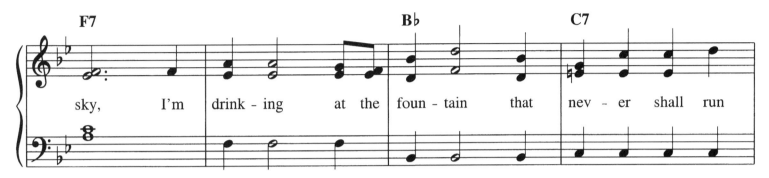

Additional Lyrics

3. Let the stormy breezes blow their cry cannot alarm me,
   I am safely sheltered here, protected by God's hand;
   Here the sun is always shining, here there's naught can harm me
   I am safe forever in Beulah Land.
   Chorus

4. Viewing here the works of God, I sink in contemplation,
   Hearing now His blessed voice, I see the way He planned;
   Dwelling in the Spirit, here I learn of full salvation
   Gladly will I tarry in Beulah Land.
   Chorus

I HAVE DECIDED TO FOLLOW JESUS

Words by an Indian Prince
Music by AUILA READ

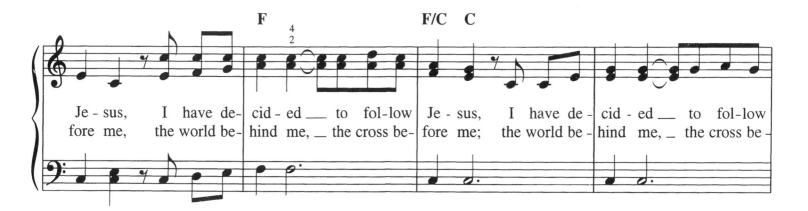

Additional Lyrics

3. Though none go with me, still I will follow, *etc.*

4. Will you decide now to follow Jesus? *etc.*

JUST A CLOSER WALK WITH THEE

Traditional
Arranged by KENNETH MORRIS

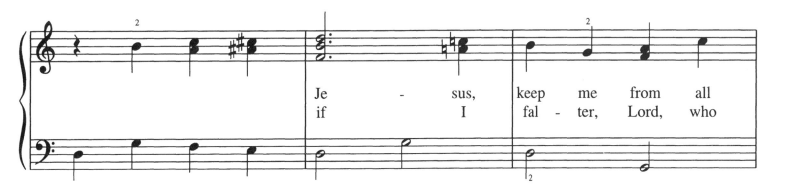

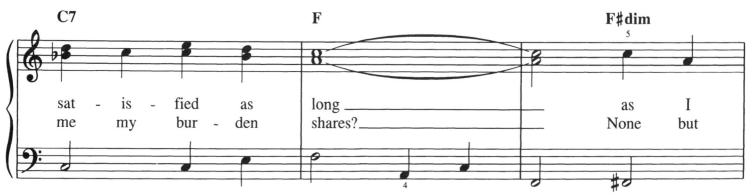

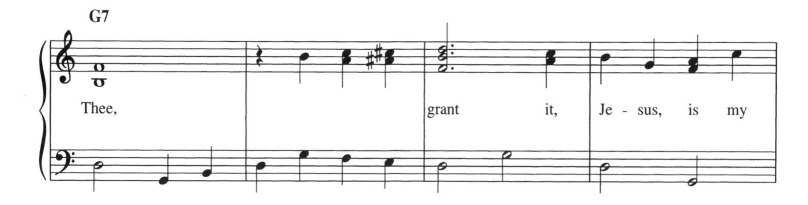

plea.＿＿＿＿＿   Dai — ly   walk - ing close to

Thee, ＿＿＿＿＿＿   let   it   be,   dear   Lord,   let   it

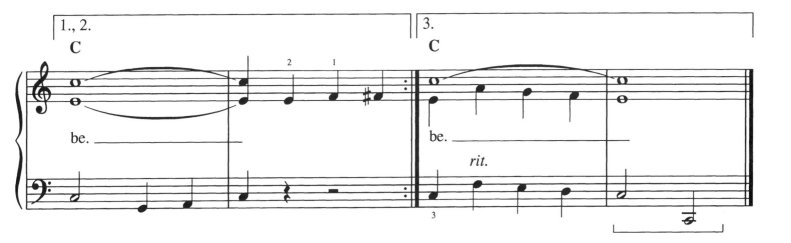

be. ＿＿＿＿＿   be. ＿＿＿＿＿

rit.

Additional Verse

3. When my feeble life is o'er,
   time for me will be no more.
   Guide me gently, safely o'er
   to Thy kingdom shore, to Thy shore.

IN THE GARDEN

Words and Music by
C. AUSTIN MILES

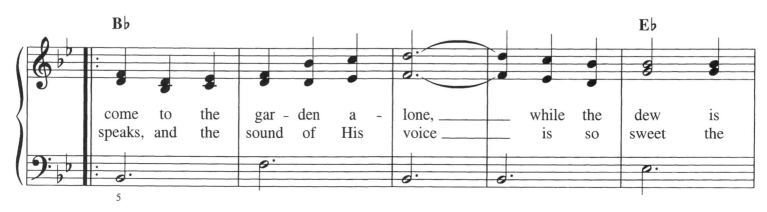

come to the gar - den a - lone,_____ while the dew is
speaks, and the sound of His voice _____ is so sweet is the

still on the ros - es; and the voice I hear, fall - ing
birds hush their sing - ing; and the mel - o - dy that He

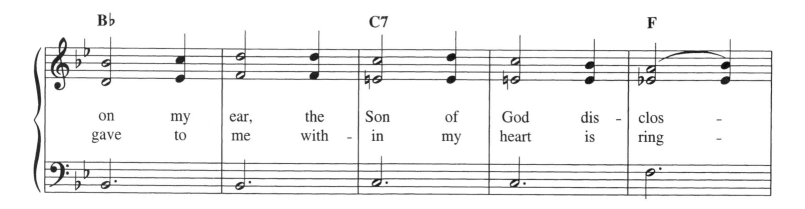

on my ear, the Son of God dis - clos -
gave to me with - in of my heart is ring -

es.
ing.} And He walks with me and He talks with me, and He

tells me I am His own; and the

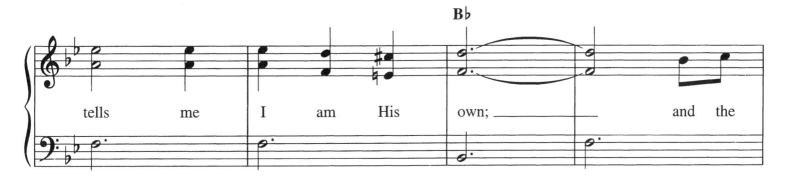

joy we share as we tar - ry there, none oth - er has

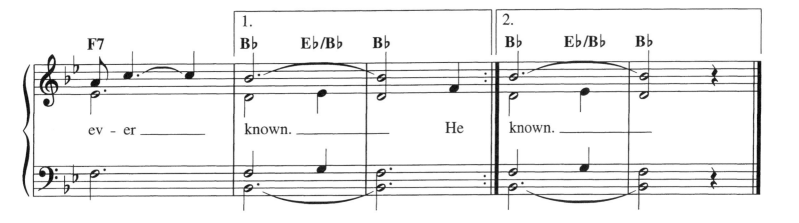

ev - er known. He known.

JUST OVER IN THE GLORYLAND

Words and Music by J.W. ACUFF
and EMMETT DEAN

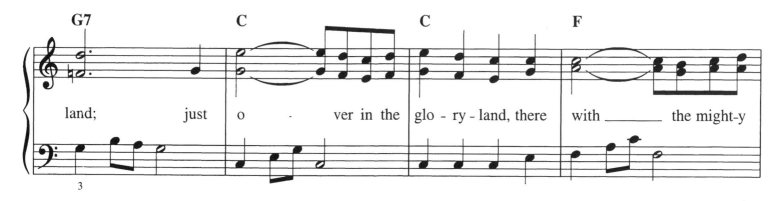

THE OLD RUGGED CROSS

By REV. GEORGE BENNARD

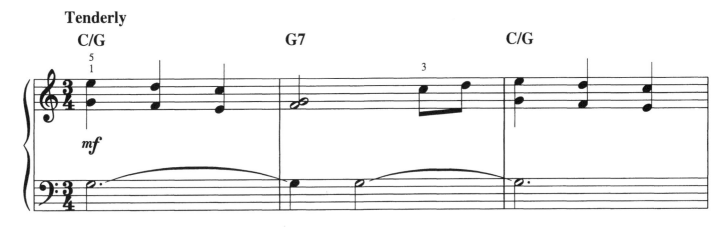

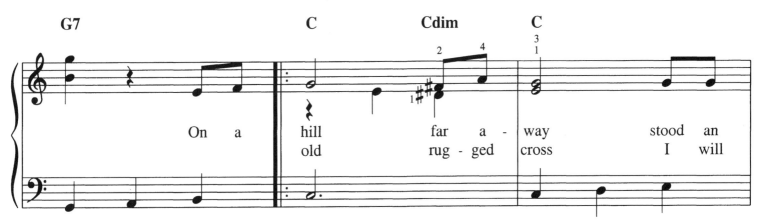

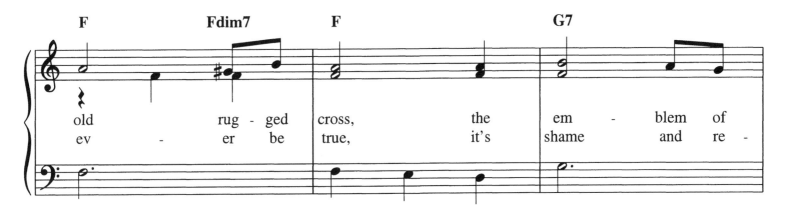

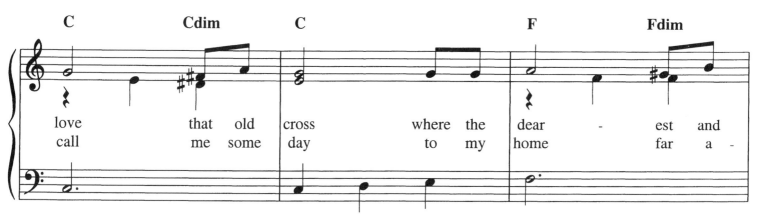

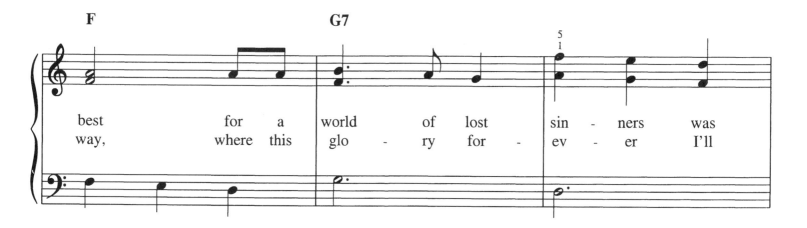

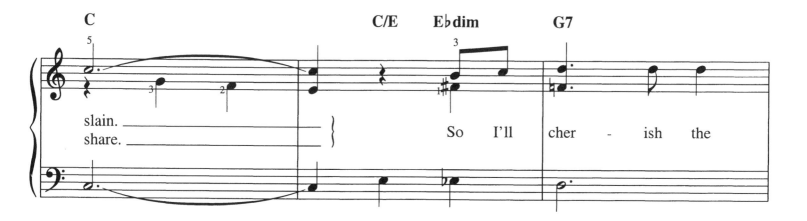

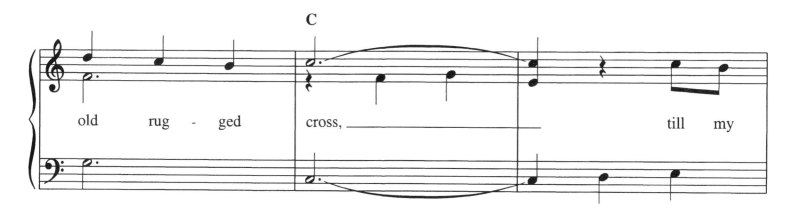

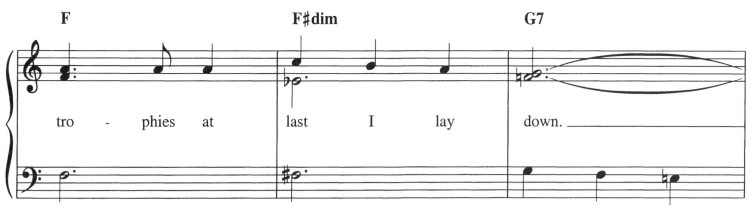

F   **F♯dim**   **G7**

tro - phies at   last I lay   down. _____

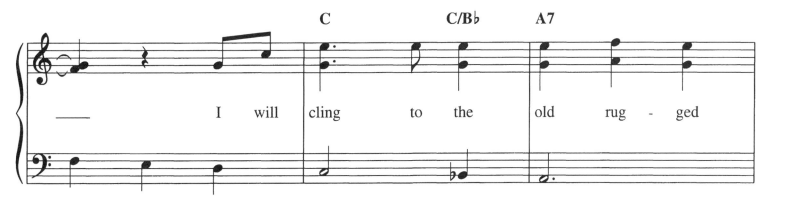

C   **C/B♭**   **A7**

_____ I will cling to the old rug - ged

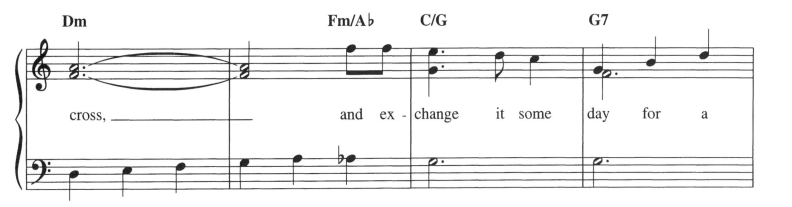

Dm   **Fm/A♭**   **C/G**   **G7**

cross, _____ and ex - change it some day for a

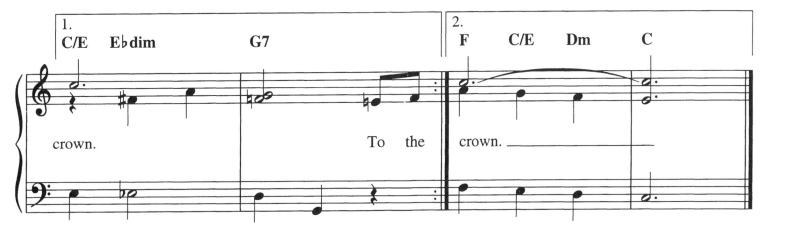

1.
C/E   **E♭dim**   **G7**

crown.   To the

2.
F   **C/E**   **Dm**   **C**

crown. _____

LEANING ON THE EVERLASTING ARMS

Words by ELISHA A. HOFFMAN
Music by ANTHONY J. SHOWALTER

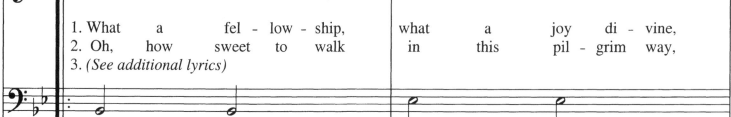

1. What a fel-low-ship, what a joy di-vine,
2. Oh, how sweet to walk in this pil-grim way,
3. (See additional lyrics)

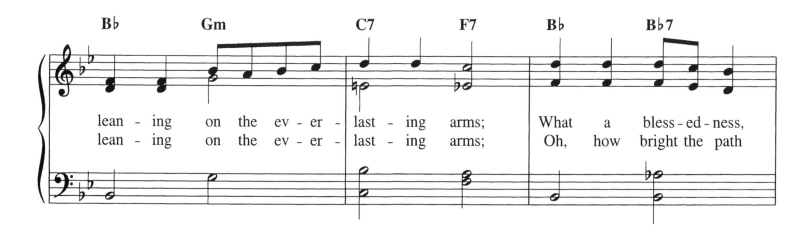

lean-ing on the ev-er-last-ing arms; What a bless-ed-ness,
lean-ing on the ev-er-last-ing arms; Oh, how bright the path

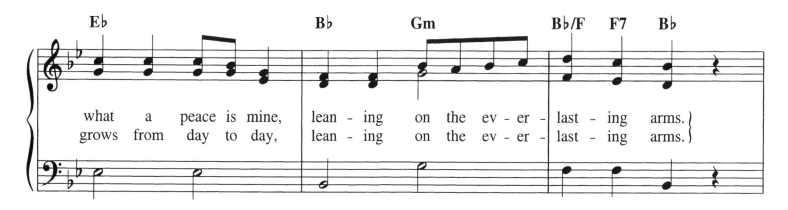

what a peace is mine, lean-ing on the ev-er-last-ing arms.}
grows from day to day, lean-ing on the ev-er-last-ing arms.}

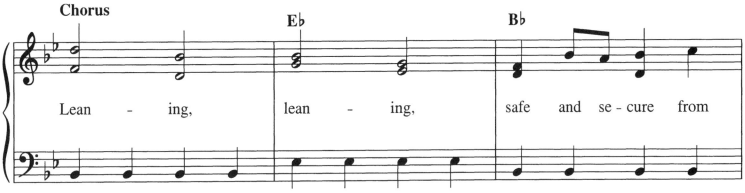

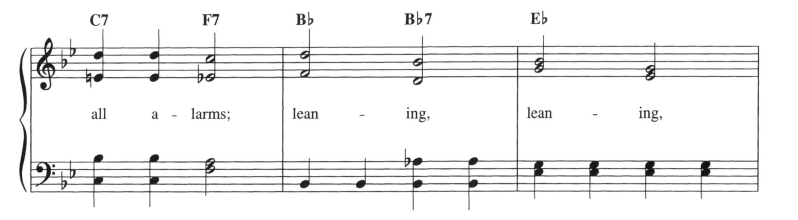

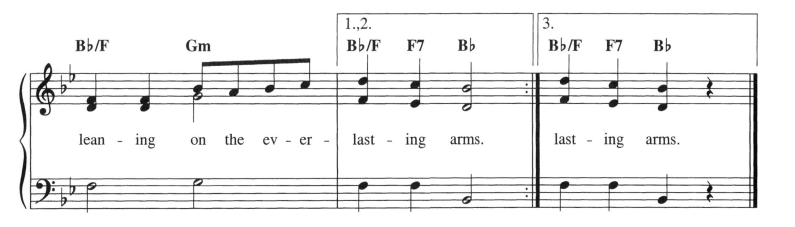

Additional Lyrics

3. What have I to dread, what have I to fear,
   Leaning on the everlasting arms?
   I have blessed peace with my Lord so near,
   Leaning on the everlasting arms.
   Chorus

LIFE'S RAILWAY TO HEAVEN

Words and Music by
M.E. ABBEY

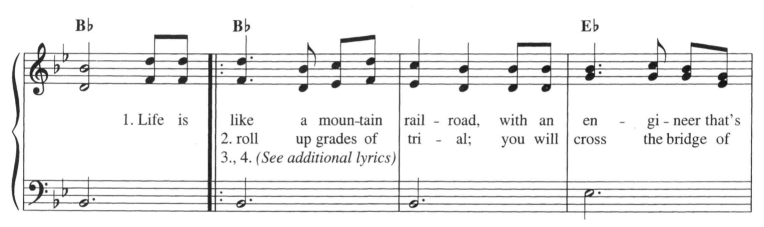

1. Life is like a moun-tain rail - road, with an en - gi - neer that's
2. roll up grades of tri - al; you will cross the bridge of
3., 4. *(See additional lyrics)*

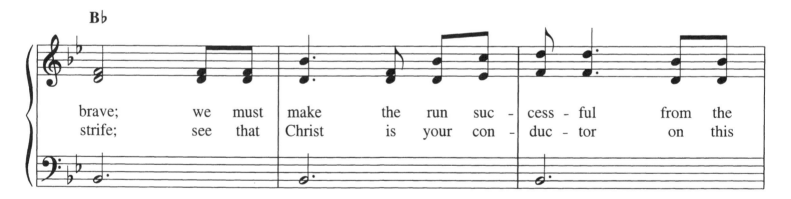

brave; we must make the run suc - cess - ful from the
strife; see that make Christ is your con - duc - tor on this

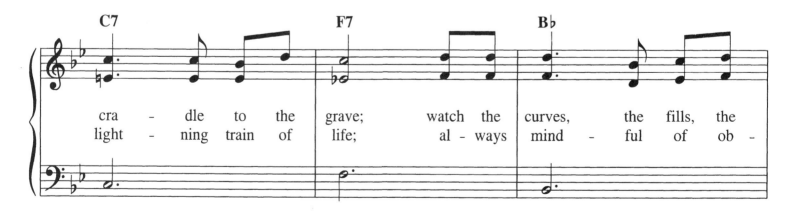

cra - dle to the grave; watch the curves, the fills, the
light - ning train of life; al - ways mind - ful of ob -

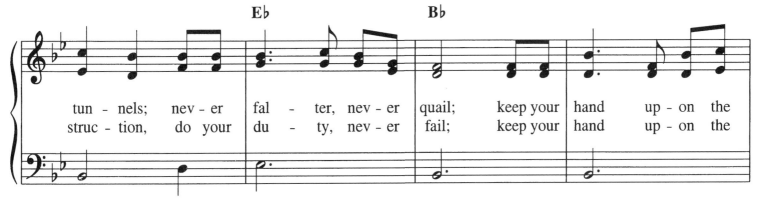

tun - nels; nev - er fal - ter, nev - er quail; keep your hand up - on the
struc - tion, do your du - ty, nev - er fail; keep your hand up - on the

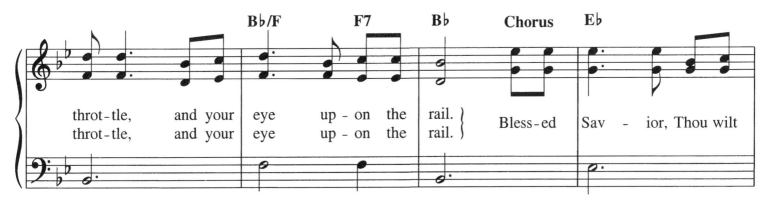

throt - tle, and your eye up - on the rail. Bless-ed Sav - ior, Thou wilt
throt - tle, and your eye up - on the rail.

guide us, Till we reach that bliss-ful shore; where the an - gels wait to

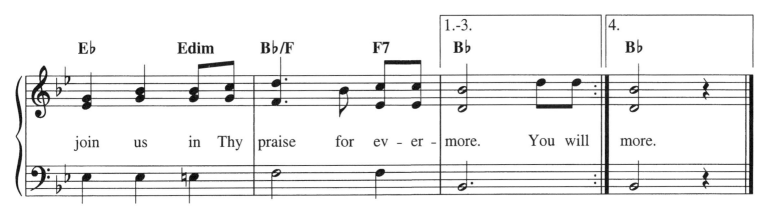

join us in Thy praise for ev - er-more. You will more.

Additional Lyrics

3. You will often find obstructions;
   Look for storms of wind and rain;
   On a fill, or curve, or trestle
   They will almost ditch your train;
   Put your trust alone in Jesus;
   Never falter, never fail;
   Keep your hand upon the throttle,
   And your eye upon the rail.
   Chorus

4. As you roll across the trestle,
   Spanning Jordan's swelling tide,
   You behold the Union Depot
   Into which your train will glide;
   There you'll meet the superintendent,
   God the Father, God the Son,
   With the hearty joyous plaudit,
   "Weary pilgrim, welcome home!"
   Chorus

THE LILY OF THE VALLEY

Words by CHARLES W. FRY
Music by WILLIAM S. HAYS

Reflectively

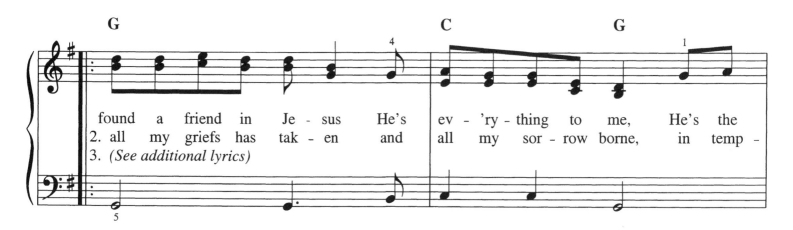

found a friend in Je - sus He's ev - 'ry - thing to me, He's the
2. all my griefs has tak - en and all my sor - row borne, in temp -
3. *(See additional lyrics)*

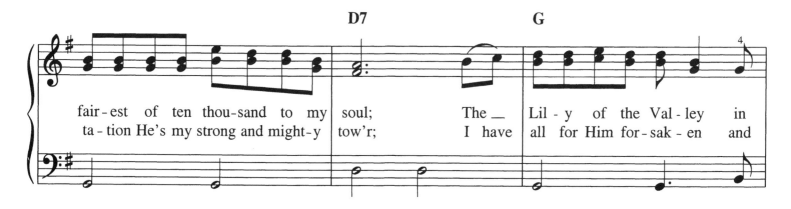

fair - est of ten thou - sand to my soul; The __ Lil - y of the Val - ley in
ta - tion He's my strong and might - y tow'r; I have all for Him for - sak - en and

Him a - lone I see all I need to cleanse and make me ful - ly
all my i - dols torn from my heart, and now He keeps me by His

whole.   In   sor-row He's my com-fort,   in   trou-ble He's my stay,   He __
pow'r.   Tho   all the world for-sake me   and   Sa - tan tempt me sore,   Thru __

tells me ev - 'ry care on Him to roll; } He's the
Je - sus I shall safe - ly reach the goal; }

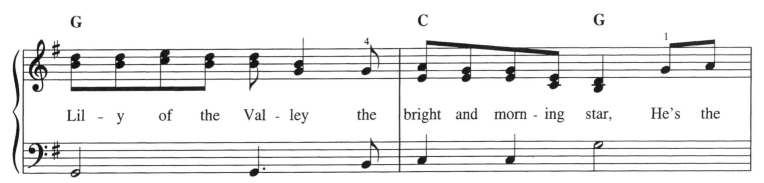

Lil - y of the Val - ley the bright and morn - ing star, He's the

fair - est of ten thou-sand to my soul.   He __ soul.

Additional Lyrics

3. He will never, never leave me nor yet forsake me here,
   While I live by faith and do His blessed will;
   A wall of fire about me, I've nothing now to fear
   With His manna He my hungry soul shall fill.
   Then sweeping up to glory I'll see His blessed face,
   Where rivers of delight shall ever roll;
   Chorus

OLD TIME RELIGION

Traditional Spiritual

Moderately

Give me that old time re-

li - gion, give me that old time re - li - gion, give me that old tiime re -

To Coda

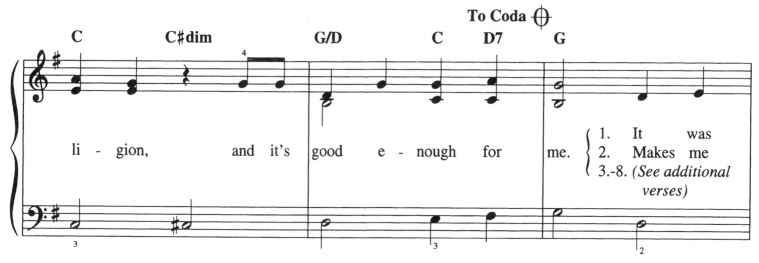

li - gion, and it's good e - nough for me.

1. It was
2. Makes me
3.-8. *(See additional verses)*

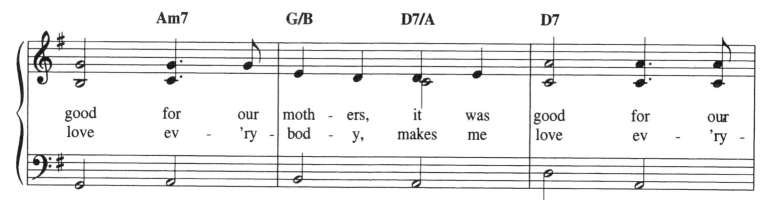

good for our moth - ers, it was good for our
love ev - 'ry - bod - y, makes me love ev - 'ry -

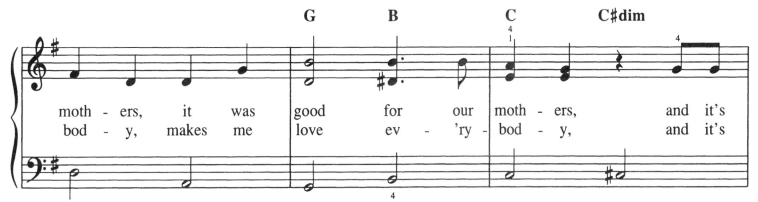

Additional Verses

3. It has saved our fathers,
   And it's good enough for me.

4. It was good for the prophet Daniel,
   And it's good enough for me.

5. It was good for the Hebrew children,
   And it's good enough for me.

6. It was tried in the fiery furnace,
   And it's good enough for me.

7. It was good for Paul and Silas,
   And it's good enough for me.

8. It will do when I am dying,
   And it's good enough for me.

ON JORDAN'S STORMY BANKS

Words by SAMUEL STENNETT
American Folk Hymn
Arranged by RIGDON M. McINTOSH

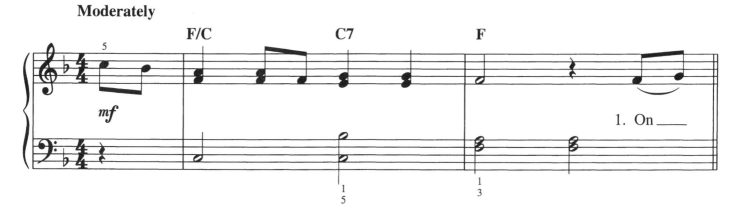

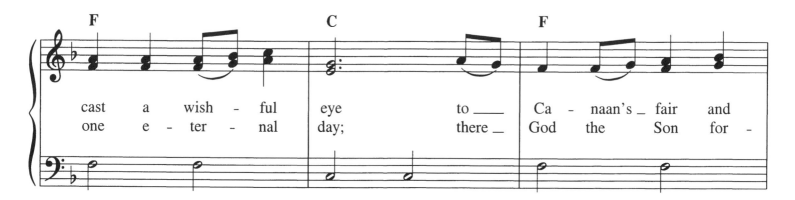

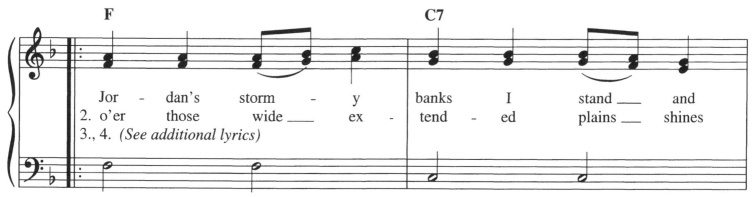

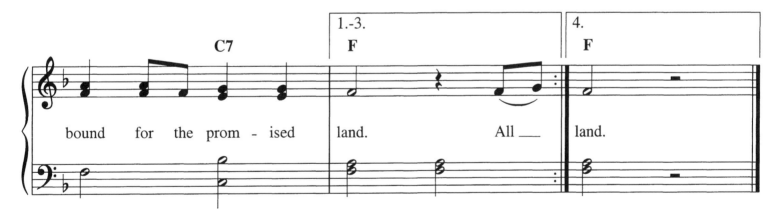

Additional Lyrics

3. No chilling winds nor pois'nous breath
   Can reach that healthful shore;
   Sickness and sorrow, pain and death
   Are felt and feared no more.
   Chorus

4. When shall I reach that happy place
   And be forever blest?
   When shall I see my Father's face
   And in His bosom rest?
   Chorus

PRECIOUS MEMORIES

Words and Music by
J.B.F. WRIGHT

Moderately slow

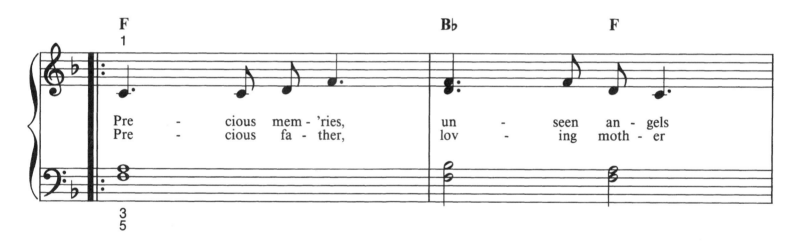

Pre - cious mem - 'ries, un - seen an - gels
Pre - cious fa - ther, lov - ing moth - er

Sent from some - where to my soul; How they lin - ger
fly a - cross the lone - ly years; And old home scenes

ev - er near me / And the sa - cred past un - fold.
of my child-hood / In fond mem - o - ry ap - pears.

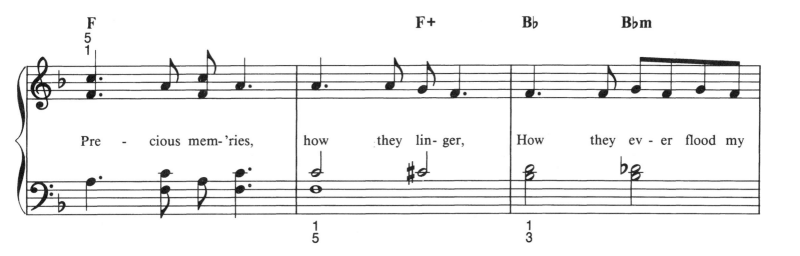

Pre - cious mem-'ries, how they lin - ger, How they ev - er flood my

soul; In the still - ness of the mid - night

pre - cious sa - cred scenes un - fold. fold.

ROCK OF AGES

Text by AUGUSTUS M. TOPLADY
Music by THOMAS HASTINGS

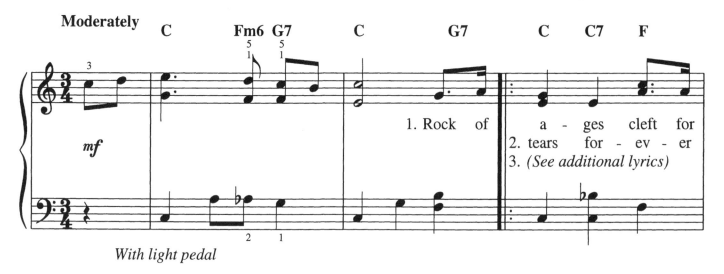

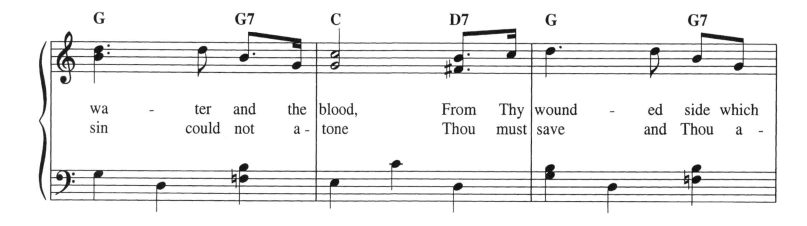

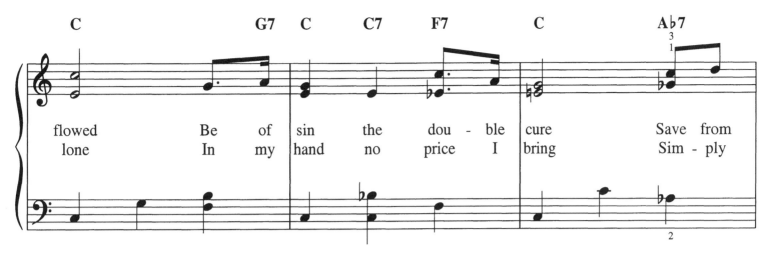

flowed   Be   of   sin   the   dou - ble   cure   Save   from
lone   In   my   hand   no   price   I   bring   Sim - ply

wrath   and   make   me   pure.   Could   my   me   Let   me
to   Thy   cross   I   cling.   While   I

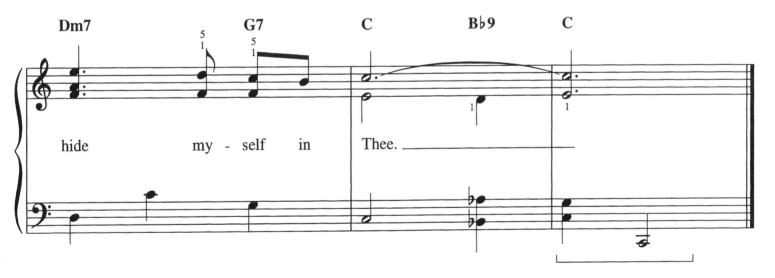

hide   my - self   in   Thee. _____

Additional Lyrics

3. While I draw this fleeting breath
    When my eyes shall close in death
    When I rise to worlds unknown
    And behold Thee on Thy throne
    Rock of Ages cleft for me
    Let me hide myself in Thee.

SHALL WE GATHER AT THE RIVER?

Words and Music by
ROBERT LOWRY

With spirit

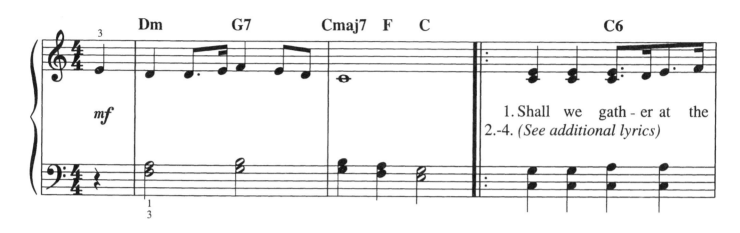

1. Shall we gath-er at the
2.-4. *(See additional lyrics)*

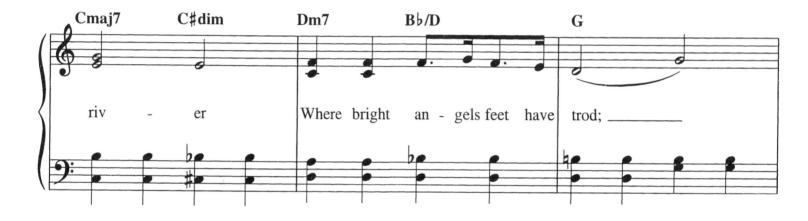

riv - er   Where bright an - gels feet have trod; _____

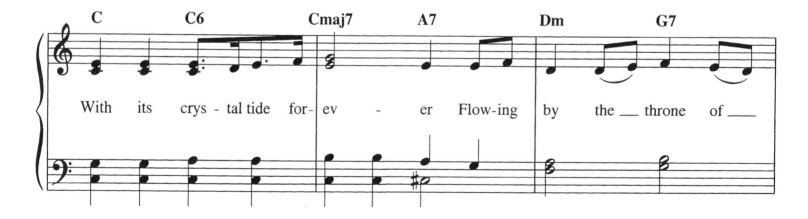

With its crys - tal tide for- ev - er Flow-ing by the ___ throne of ___

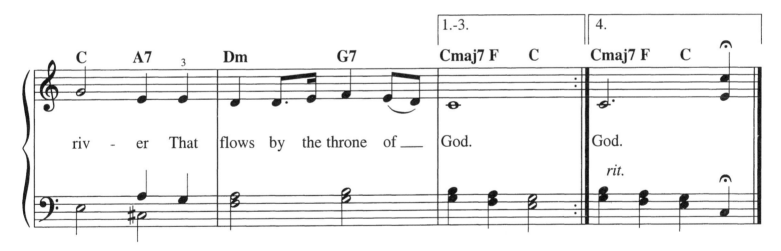

Additional Lyrics

2. On the bosom of the river,
Where the Savior King we own,
We shall meet, and sorrow never,
'Neath the glory of the throne.
Refrain

3. Ere we reach the shining river,
Lay we every burden down;
Grace our spirits will deliver,
And provide a robe and crown.
Refrain

4. Soon we'll reach the shining river,
Soon our pilgrimage will cease;
Soon our happy hearts will quiver
With the melody of peace.
Refrain

SINCE JESUS CAME INTO MY HEART

Words by R.H. McDANIEL
Music by CHARLES H. GABRIEL

Joyfully

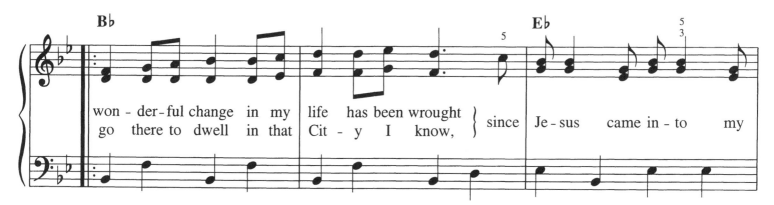

Je - sus came in - to my heart, since

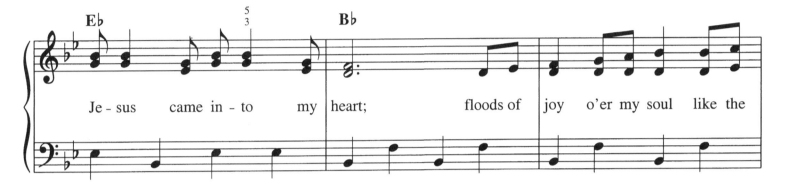

Je - sus came in - to my heart; floods of joy o'er my soul like the

sea bil - lows roll, since Je - sus came in - to my heart. I shall

heart, since Je - sus came in - to my heart.

SWEET BY AND BY

Words by SANFORD FILLMORE BENNETT
Music by JOSEPH P. WEBSTER

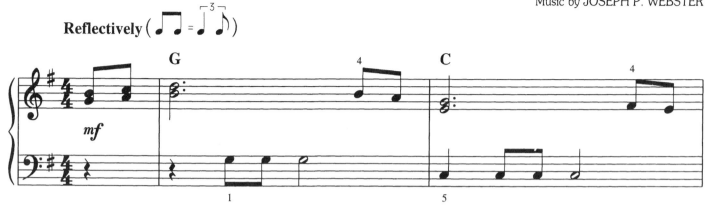

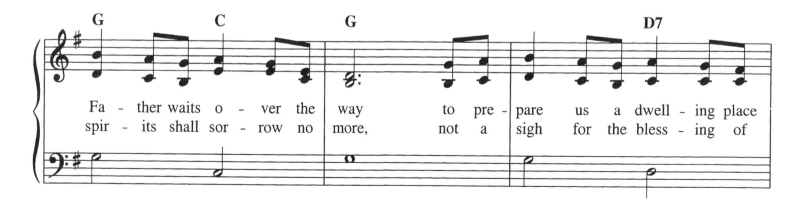

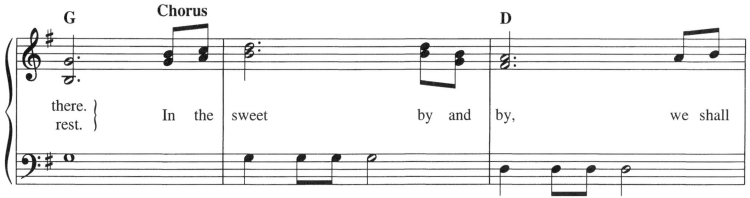

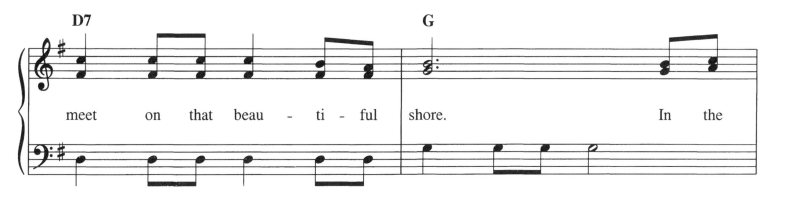

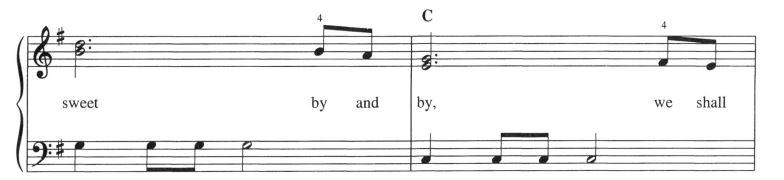

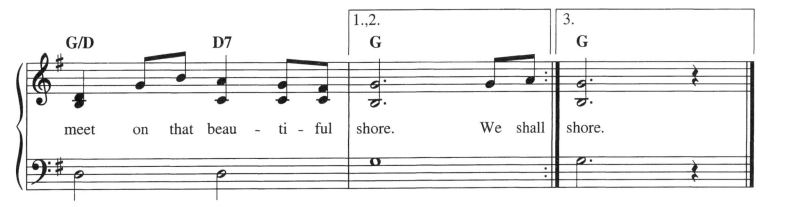

Additional Lyrics

3. To our bountiful Father above
   We will offer our tribute of praise,
   For the glorious gift of His love
   And the blessings that hallow our days.
   Chorus

THERE IS A FOUNTAIN

Words by WILLIAM COWPER
Traditional American Melody
Arranged by LOWELL MASON

Gently

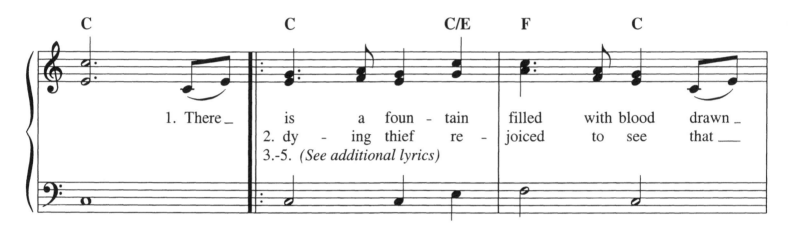

1. There _ is a foun - tain filled with blood drawn _
2. dy - ing thief re - joiced to see that __
3.-5. *(See additional lyrics)*

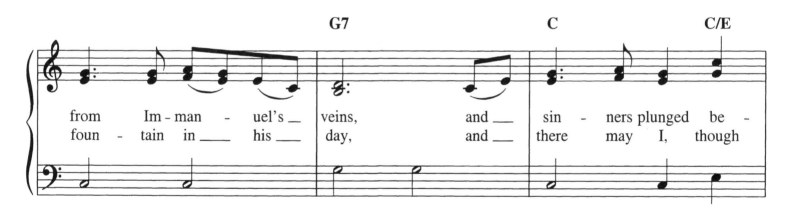

from Im - man - uel's _ veins, and _ sin - ners plunged be -
foun - tain in __ his __ day, and __ there may I, though

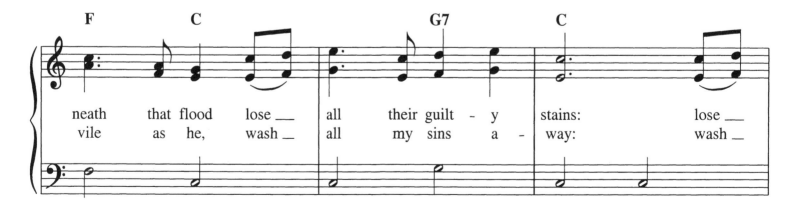

neath that flood lose __ all their guilt - y stains: lose __
vile as he, wash __ all my sins a - way: wash __

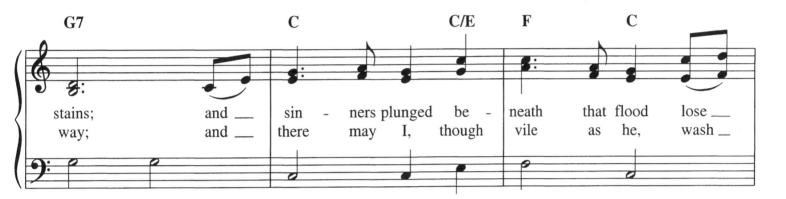

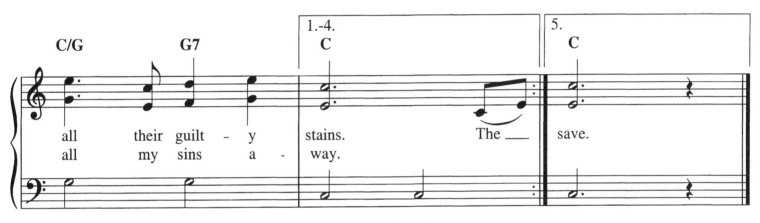

Additional Lyrics

3. Dear dying Lamb, Thy precious blood
    Shall never lose its pow'r,
    Till all the ransomed Church of God
    Be saved to sin no more:
    Be saved to sin no more,
    Be saved to sin no more.
    Till all the ransomed Church of God
    Be saved to sin no more.

4. E'er since, by faith, I saw the stream
    Thy flowing wounds supply,
    Redeeming love has been my theme
    And shall be till I die:
    And shall be till I die,
    And shall be till I die.
    Redeeming love has been my theme
    And shall be till I die.

5. When this poor lisping, stamm'ring tongue
    Lies silent in the grave,
    Then in a nobler, sweeter song
    I'll sing Thy pow'r to save;
    I'll sing Thy pow'r to save,
    I'll sing Thy pow'r to save.
    Then in a nobler, sweeter song
    I'll sing Thy pow'r to save.

THERE IS POWER IN THE BLOOD

Words and Music by
LEWIS E. JONES

Moderately fast

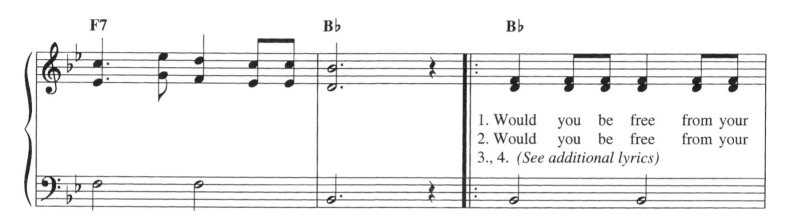

1. Would you be free from your
2. Would you be free from your
3., 4. *(See additional lyrics)*

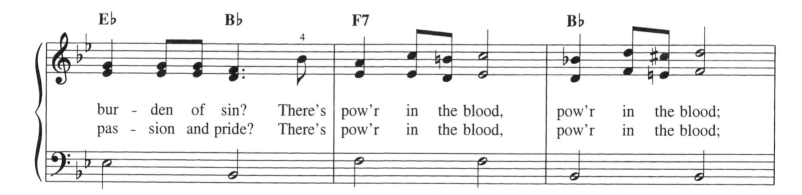

bur - den of sin? There's pow'r in the blood, pow'r in the blood;
pas - sion and pride? There's pow'r in the blood, pow'r in the blood;

would you o'er e - vil a vic - to - ry win? } There's
come for a cleans - ing to Cal - va - ry's tide. }

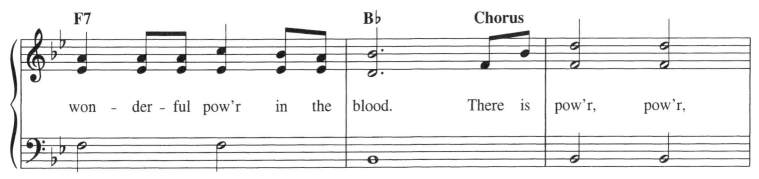

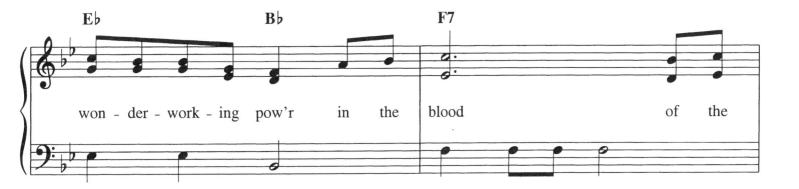

Additional Lyrics

3. Would you be whiter, much whiter than snow?
   There's pow'r in the blood, pow'r in the blood;
   Sin-stains are lost in its live-giving flow.
   There's wonderful pow'r in the blood.
   Chorus

4. Would you do service for Jesus your King?
   There's pow'r in the blood, pow'r in the blood;
   Would you live daily His praises to sing?
   There's wonderful pow'r in the blood.
   Chorus

WE'LL UNDERSTAND IT BETTER BY AND BY

Words and Music by
CHARLES A. TINDLEY

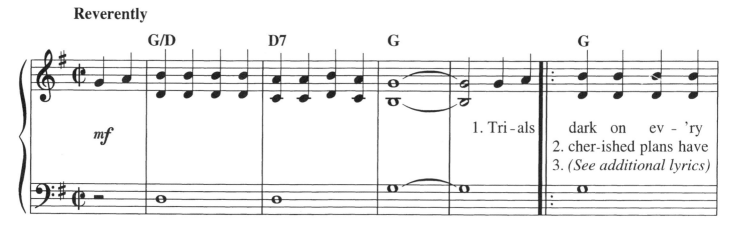

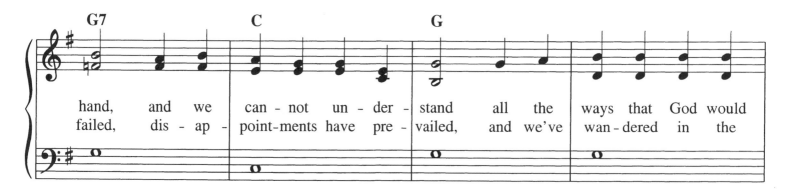

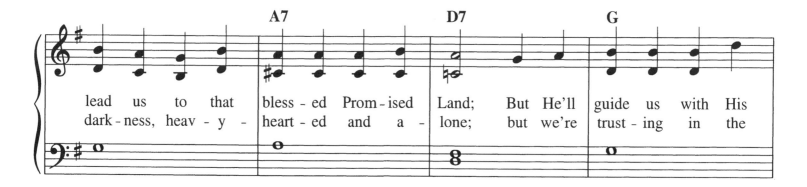

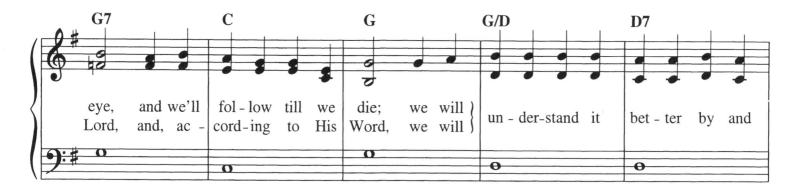

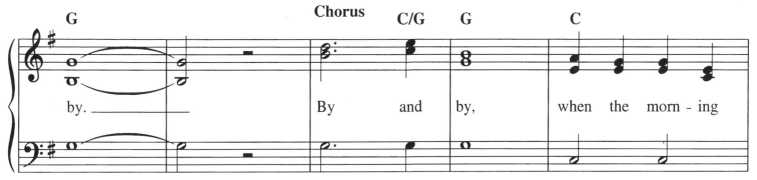

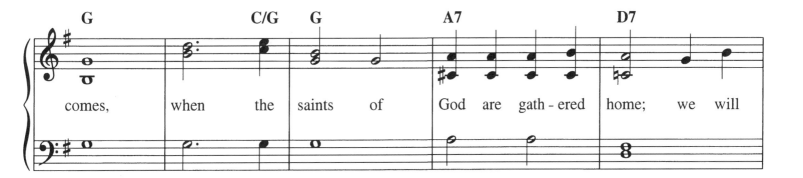

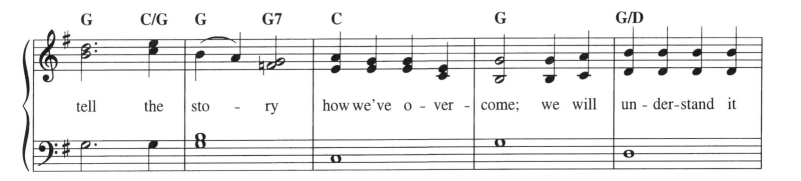

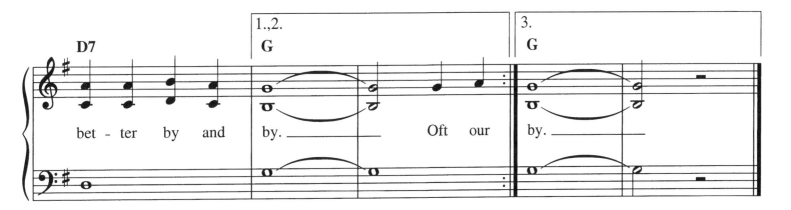

Additional Lyrics

3. Temptations, hidden snares often take us unawares
   And our hearts are made to bleed for some thoughtless word or deed,
   And we wonder why the test when we try to do our best, but we'll
   Understand it better by and by.
   Chorus

WHAT A FRIEND WE HAVE IN JESUS

Words by JOSEPH SCRIVEN
Music by CHARLES C. CONVERSE

Slowly

1. What a friend we have in
2. Have we tri - als and temp -
3. *(See additional verses)*

Je - sus, all our sins and griefs to bear!
ta - tions? Is there trou-ble an - y- where?

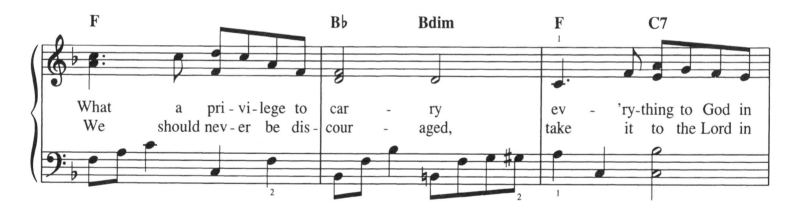

What a pri - vi-lege to car - ry ev - 'ry-thing to God in
We should nev - er be dis- cour - aged, take it to the Lord in

prayer! Oh, what peace we of - ten for - feit,
prayer! Can we find a friend so faith - ful,

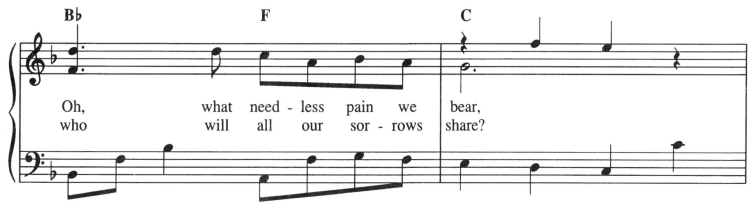

Oh, what need-less pain we bear,
who will all our sor-rows share?

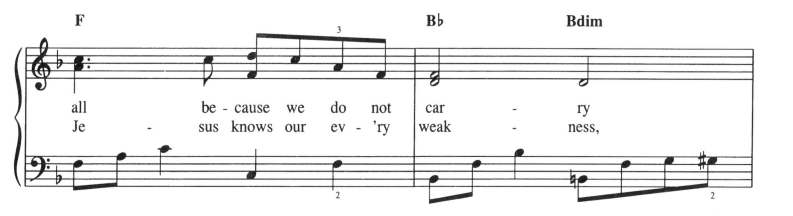

all be-cause we do not car - ry
Je - sus knows our ev-'ry weak - ness,

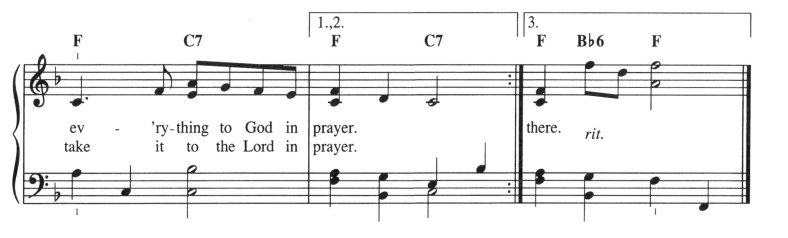

ev - 'ry-thing to God in prayer.
take it to the Lord in prayer.

there. *rit.*

Additional Verse

3. Are we weak and heavy-laden,
cumbered with a load of care?
Precious Savior, still our refuge:
take it to the Lord in prayer.
Do thy friends despise, forsake thee?
Take it to the Lord in prayer:
In His arms He'll take and shield thee,
thou wilt find a solace there.

WHEN THE ROLL IS CALLED UP YONDER

Words and Music by
JAMES M. BLACK

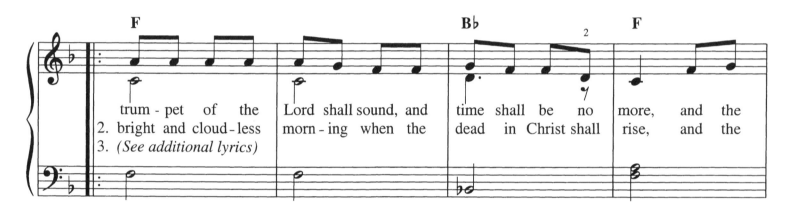

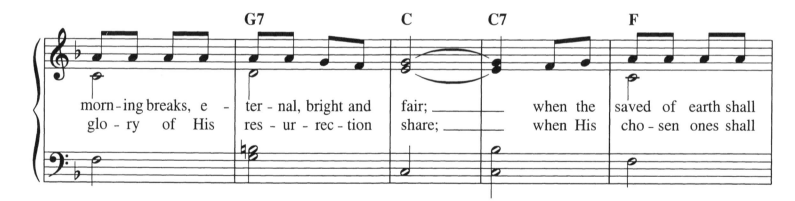

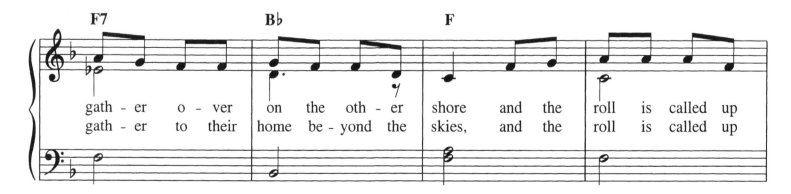

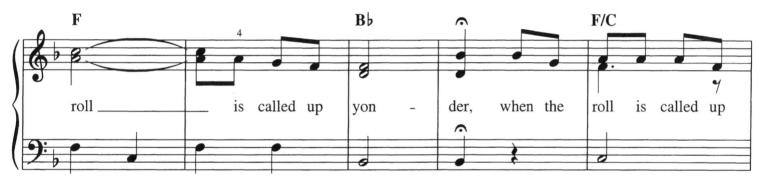

Additional Lyrics

3. Let us labor for the Master from the dawn till setting sun,
   Let us talk of all His wondrous love and care;
   Then when all of life is over and our work on earth is done
   And the roll is called up yonder, I'll be there!
   Chorus

WHEN WE ALL GET TO HEAVEN

Words and Music by E.E. HEWITT
and J.G. WILSON

Moderately

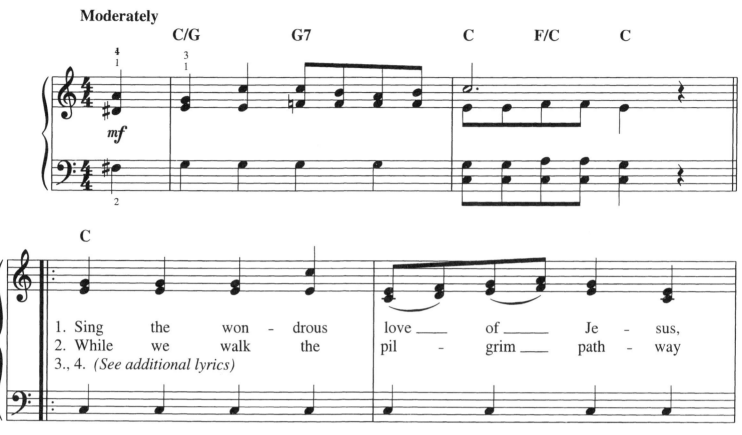

1. Sing the won-drous love ___ of ___ Je - sus,
2. While we walk the pil - grim ___ path - way
3., 4. *(See additional lyrics)*

sing His mer - cy ___ and His grace; in the man - sions
clouds will o - ver - spread the sky; but when trav - 'ling

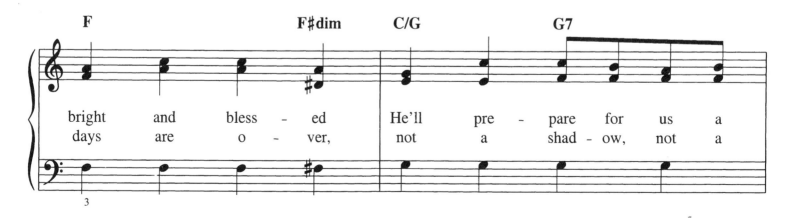

bright and bless - ed He'll pre - pare for us a
days are o - ver, not a shad - ow, not a

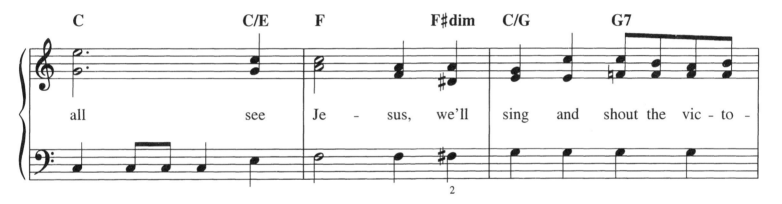

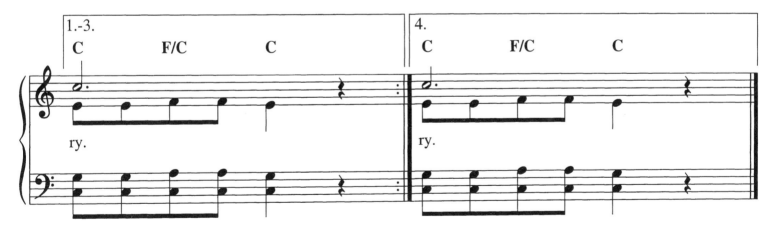

Additional Lyrics

3. Let us then be true and faithful,
   Trusting, serving every day;
   Just one glimpse of Him in glory
   Will the toils of life repay.
   Chorus

4. Onward to the prize before us!
   Soon His beauty we'll behold;
   Soon the pearly gates will open,
   We shall tread the streets of gold.
   Chorus

SWEET HOUR OF PRAYER

Words by WILLIAM W. WALFORD
Music by WILLIAM B. BRADBURY

Gently

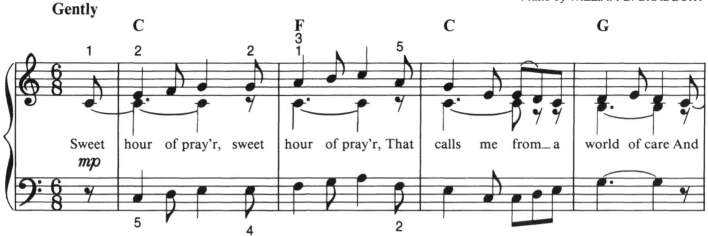

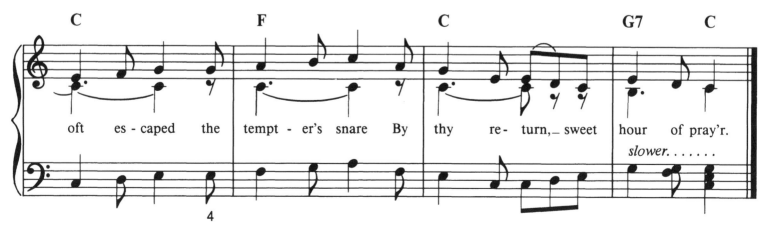

WHISPERING HOPE

Words and Music by
ALICE HAWTHORNE

Gently, lilting

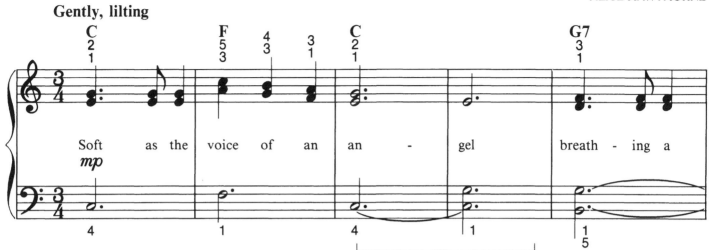

Soft as the voice of an an - gel breath - ing a

les - son un - heard, _____ Hope with a gen - tle per -

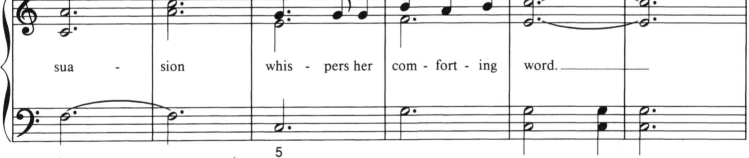

sua - sion whis - pers her com - fort - ing word. _____

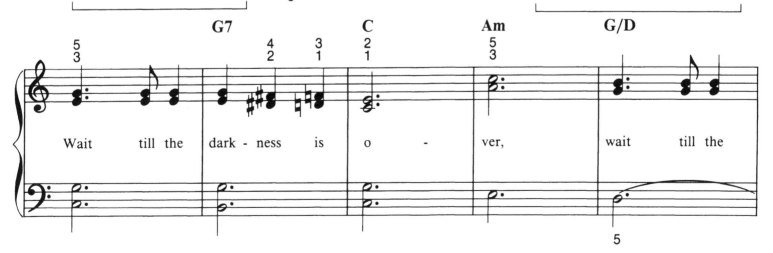

Wait till the dark - ness is o - ver, wait till the

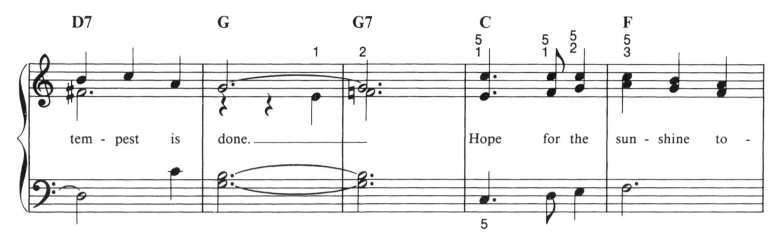

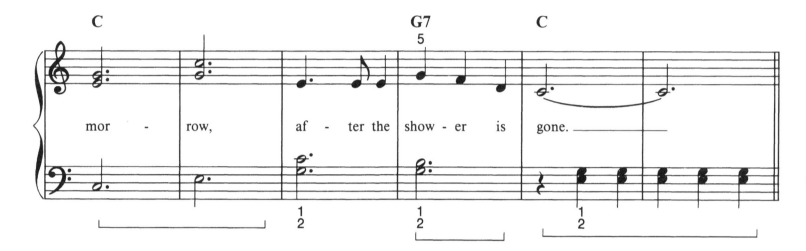

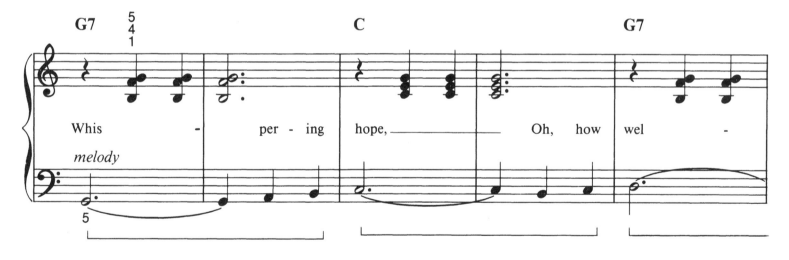

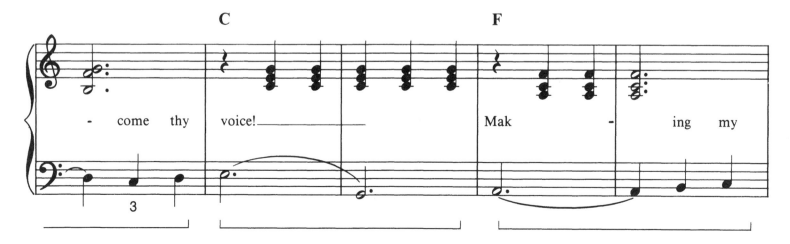

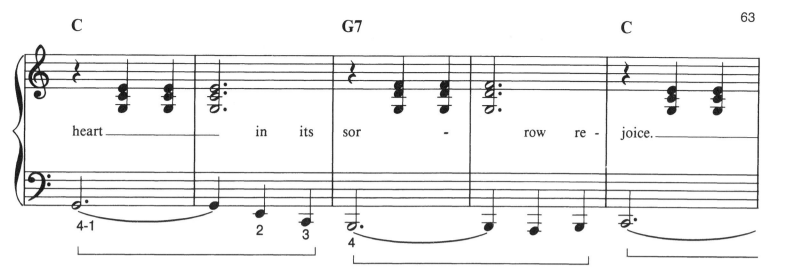

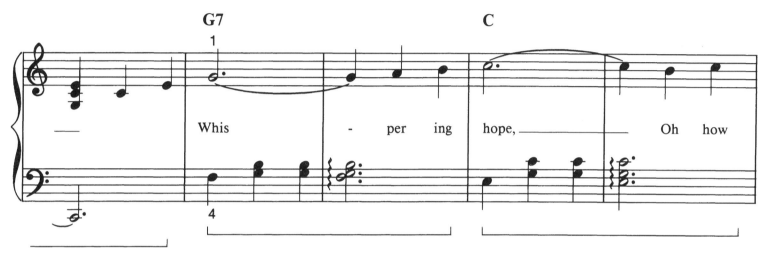

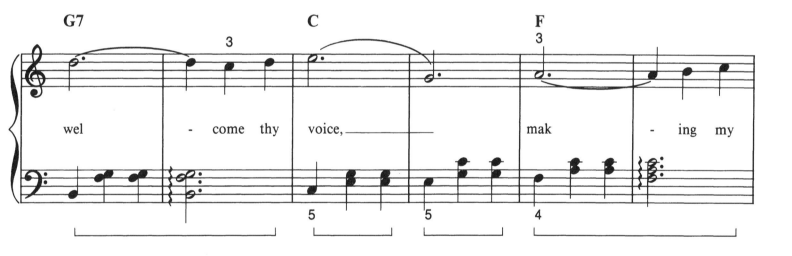

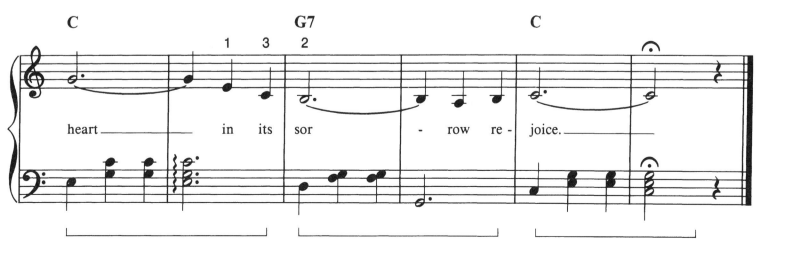